Euphemisms That Get on My You-Know-Whats

Euphemisms That Get on My You-Know-Whats

And Other Meticulously Assembled Lists of Extremely Valuable Nonsense

Adam Sharp

Andrews McMeel
PUBLISHING®

Euphemisms That Get on My You-Know-Whats

Andrews McMeel Publishing
a division of Andrews McMeel Universal
1130 Walnut Street, Kansas City, Missouri 64106
www.andrewsmcmeel.com

21 22 23 24 25 SDB 10 9 8 7 6 5 4 3 2 1

ISBN: 978-1-5248-7010-2

Library of Congress Control Number: 2021934840

First published as *The Correct Order of Biscuits* in Great Britain in 2020 by Trapeze, an imprint of The Orion Publishing Group Ltd.

3\. *For my dad, who loved lists also*

2\. *For my granddad, who raised me*

1\. *For my mum, who was gone too soon*

3. "If people did not sometimes do silly things, nothing intelligent would ever get done."

   —Ludwig Wittgenstein

2. "To appreciate nonsense requires a serious interest in life."

   —Gelett Burgess

1. "List, list, O, list!"

   —William Shakespeare

INTRODUCTION

A list of options for the introduction

5. A lengthy anecdote about the time, while still in diapers, that I wrote my first ever list

4. An essay on why I love lists so much (which cleverly implies that I'm the world's leading listologist)

3. A look at the psychology of list-making (is my list-making compulsion related to the Oedipus complex? OCD? Could I have tendencies toward serial killing?)

2. A look at some great lists/list-makers throughout history (Moses, for example, was super into them)

1. Just get on with it

A list of New Year's resolutions

1. Make longer lists

A list of the worst lyrics ever conceived

7. You look fresh like a salad, so smooth (BTS)
6. Are we human, or are we dancer? (The Killers)
5. Even food don't taste that good (Bryan Adams)
4. I'm as serious as cancer, when I say rhythm is a dancer (Snap)
3. Life, oh life, oh life, oh life (Des'ree)*
2. Like a tramp in the night, I was begging for you (Samantha Fox)
1. Santa's on his sleigh, but now he's two meters away (Robbie Williams)†

---

* The Des'ree song "Life" also boasts the immortal lines, "I don't want to see a ghost / It's a sight that I fear most / I'd rather have a piece of toast."

† This comes from Robbie Williams's COVID-19 Christmas song, "Can't Stop Christmas," which also includes lines such as "Sadly some friends disappeared / It's never been like this before (ooh, ooh)" and "If you're wondering what I like / Stacks of sanitizer will do fine."

A list of how dogs go woof woof in different languages (a ruff approximation)

8. Voff voff (Icelandic)

7. Lol lol (Tamil)

6. Bup bup (Catalan)

5. Ham ham (Albanian)

4. Woke woke (Burmese)

3. Gong gong (Malay)

2. Wang wang (Mandarin)

1. Bawf (Scots)

A list of words that sound rude but aren't

10. Fallacious

9. Kumquat

8. Penal

7. Cleat

6. Succulent

5. Titular

4. Gesticulate

3. Rectory

2. Manhole

1. Pumpkin (vegetable or incest?)

A list of English Regency slang

8. Dicked in the knob (crazy)
7. The apple dumplin' shop (breasts)
6. Lapping your congo (drinking tea)
5. The mulligrubs (feeling down)
4. A jaw-me-dead (a talkative person)
3. Irish apricots (potatoes)
2. Killing the canary (avoiding work)
1. My arse on a bandbox (like hell I will)

A list of Kim Jong-il's achievements (according to his official biography)

7. Learned to walk (three weeks old)
6. Learned to talk (eight weeks old)
5. Wrote 1,500 books and six full operas (in college)
4. Shot eleven holes-in-one in a golf game
3. Controlled the weather with his mind
2. Invented the hamburger
1. Never had to poop

A list of things I feared as a kid but now rarely worry about

8. Quicksand
7. Laser beams
6. The Bog of Eternal Stench
5. Daleks
4. Venus flytraps
3. Spontaneous combustion
2. Knight Rider getting canceled
1. The wind changing and my face getting stuck that way*

---

* You may be thinking that's quite a short list, and I was some serious badass as a child, but alas, there were plenty of other things I feared—such as sharks in swimming pools, stepping on cracks in the pavement, holding on to a balloon too long and floating away with it, Miss May (scary art teacher), Venger from *Dungeons & Dragons*, a tree growing inside my stomach (from swallowing apple seeds), the Bermuda Triangle, railway lines, piranhas, rabies, acid rain, moths, and, finally, scarecrows—which, unlike the rest of the list, still terrify me to this day.

A list of things I never worried about as a kid that terrify me as an adult

7. Parties
6. Talking to people at parties
5. Loud neighbors moving in (and having parties)
4. Dying alone
3. Making grammatical errors
2. People standing too close
1. Keanu Reeves turning out to be evil

A list of the top ten greatest animals ever

10. Animals
9. Are
8. Sentient
7. Beings
6. Not
5. Objects
4. To
3. Be
2. Ranked
1. Penguins*†

* Why penguins rule, part 823: In the 1990s, a king penguin called Lala was rescued from a fishing net by the Nishimoto family. They built him his own air-conditioned room, and he was even trained to waddle into town to collect groceries (wearing a specially made Pingu backpack).

† Why penguins rule, part 967: In 2011, a retired bricklayer, João Pereira de Souza, found a Magellanic penguin covered in oil. He nursed the penguin (who he named Dindim) back to health, and every year since, Dindim has returned to visit him (because penguins are the greatest!).

A list of tribute act names*

7. By Jovi (Bon Jovi)
6. Gwen in Doubt (Gwen Stefani and No Doubt)
5. Cheap Purple (Deep Purple)
4. Sgt. Pepper's Only Dart Board Band (The Beatles)
3. Petty Theft (Tom Petty)
2. Earth, Wind for Hire (Earth, Wind & Fire)
1. Amy Housewine (Amy Winehouse)

A bonus list of suggested names for vegan cover bands

5. The Tofu Fighters (The Foo Fighters)
4. QuoЯn (KoЯn)
3. Rage Against the Sardine (Rage Against the Machine)
2. Noah and the Whaling Ban (Noah and the Whale)
1. Soy Division (Joy Division)

---

* If ever I'm in a Fleetwood Mac tribute act, I will insist we be called Fleetwood PC (and our business cards will say, "nowhere near as good but much cheaper").

A list of Victorian slang

8. Gigglemug (always smiling)

7. Scandal water (tea)

6. Bitch the pot (pour the tea)

5. Got the morbs (temporary sadness)

4. Tight as a boiled owl (drunk)

3. Poked up (embarrassed)

2. Sauce-box (the mouth)

1. Not up to dick (unwell)

A list of things greedy people want in different languages

7. To have their cake and eat it (English)
6. To have the porridge and the mustache (Tamil)
5. To dance at two weddings (German)
4. To sit on two horses with one backside (Hungarian)
3. To have the butter, the money to buy the butter, and a smile from the milkmaid (French)
2. To have a cask full of wine and a drunk wife (Italian)
1. To eat a fish and sit on a dick (Russian)*

* And there is one more phrase—"Me want cookie and me want more cookie"—in Cookie Monsterish.

A list of ideas for ad slogans

8. We'll drive you up the wall (stairlift installer)
7. Our business is going down the drain (plumber)
6. Our days are numbered (calendar maker)
5. We always keep it up (airline)
4. Bringing out your inner child (maternity ward)
3. Our clients speak very highly of us (helium manufacturer)
2. We're not afraid to raise a few eyebrows (plastic surgeons)
1. Summer special: Smoking hot body or your money back (crematorium)

A list of (understandably) forgotten proverbs from around the world

5. One should not board a ship without an onion (Dutch)

4. She is a foolish woman who blames her own cabbage (Danish)

3. One must let people talk sense since fish can't (Polish)

2. Sometimes, one must let turnips be pears (German)

1. Never bolt your door with a boiled carrot (Irish)

A list of reasons to love Norway

3. In Norway, Mr. Bump from the Mr. Men children's books is called Herr Dumpidump

2. Norwegians use the word texas to mean batshit crazy (as in "Florida is totally texas!")

1. The Colonel-in-Chief of the Norwegian King's Guard, Brigadier Sir Nils Olav III, is a penguin

A list of names for a couch potato from different languages

5. House cockerel (Ghanaian Ewe)
4. Couch pig (Norwegian)
3. Armchair fungus (Flemish)
2. Sofa turd (Chilean Spanish)
1. One who squats in the parlor (German)

A list of bands in order of efficacy

3. Placebo
2. The Cure
1. Prevention

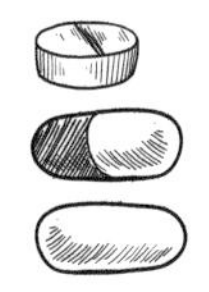

A list of names for bookworms from around the world

7. Book flea (Indonesian)
6. Book tree (Yoruba)
5. Book maggot (Finnish)*
4. Library mouse (Romanian)
3. Read-rat (German)
2. Reading horse (Danish)
1. Ink drinker (French)†

---

* OK fine—it's technically "reading larva/caterpillar."

† The most well-known term for a bookworm in France is *rat de bibliothèque* (library rat). But my grandmother, who grew up in Ardes in Auvergne-Rhône-Alpes, would often refer to a bookworm as a *buveur d'encre* (ink drinker). I originally thought it was another one of her made-up phrases, but I have since spoken to other people from her region who use it (and there is even a bookshop in Paris called Les Buveurs d'encre). So, Nicole Lefevre, this list is dedicated to you.

A list of animal rhymes you can use to say farewell

8. In a while, crocodile
7. Toodle-oo, kangaroo
6. Ciao for now, Jersey cow
5. Why you still here, white-tailed deer
4. Just piss off, gypsy moth
3. Go to hell, red gazelle
2. Kiss my hole, woodland vole
1. Off you fuck, crested duck

A list of films to watch if you like pasta

5. *A Fusilli Good Men*
4. *The Grand Budapesto Hotel*
3. *Lawrence of Arrabiata*
2. *Fear and Loathing in Lasagne*
1. *The Texas Chainsaw Marinara*

A bonus list of books to read if you like pasta

5. *Love in the Time of Carbonara*
4. *Pi-gnocchi-o*
3. *A Tagliatelle of Two Cities*
2. *The Heart is a Cannelloni Hunter*
1. *Remembrance of Things Pasta*

A list of celebrity rhymes you can use to say farewell

8. Come again soon, Reese Witherspoon
7. Have a nice day, Lana Del Rey
6. See you anon, Simon Le Bon
5. There's the door, Pauly Shore
4. Now off you feck, Gregory Peck
3. Take a hike, Dick Van Dyke
2. Fall down a well, Harvey Keitel
1. I've run out of rhymes, Beyoncé

A list of international expressions for being pregnant

7. Rearing tiny bones (Welsh)
6. To be two-souled (Georgian)
5. A pearl forming in a clamshell (Mandarin)
4. A marionette in the drawer (French)
3. A bun in the oven (English)
2. A roast in the oven (German)
1. Carrying a burden (Russian)*

A bonus list of the titles for the movie *Knocked Up* around the world

5. *Slightly Pregnant* (Peru)
4. *A Little Bit Pregnant* (Russia)
3. *A Huge Bummer* (Portugal)
2. *One Night, Big Belly* (China)
1. *The Date That Screwed Me* (Israel)

---

* There's an even blunter expression in Spanish that usually refers to someone putting on weight in general, but I've heard it used in reference to pregnancy. It's "to become like a ham."

A list of things that are technically illegal in England

8. Operating a cow while drunk
7. Flying a kite in the street
6. Carrying planks of wood (in London)
5. Shaking your doormat (after 8:00 a.m.)
4. Singing "Happy Birthday" (ever)
3. Sliding on ice or snow
2. Wearing a suit of armor in Parliament
1. Holding a salmon in "suspicious circumstances"

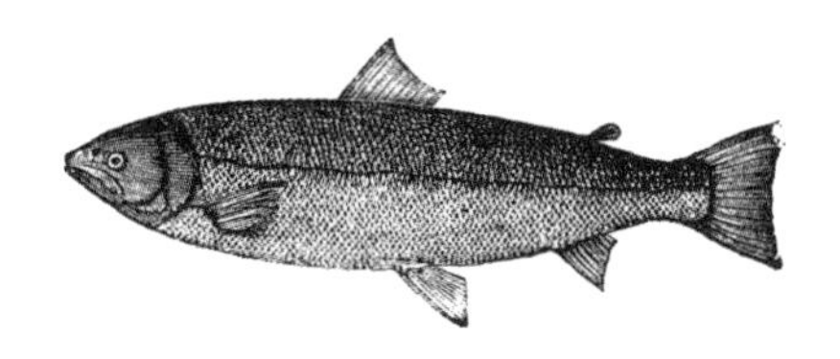

A list of sensible laws from around the world

5. In Arizona, it is illegal to let a donkey sleep in your bathtub
4. In Turin, local council law states you must walk your dog at least three times a day
3. In Blythe, California, you're not allowed to wear cowboy boots unless you own at least two cows
2. In Queensland, it's illegal to own a rabbit unless you're a magician
1. In Switzerland, you cannot own just one guinea pig*

* Guinea pigs are social animals, and it's deemed cruel to deprive them of the company of other guinea pigs. Swiss law also protects parrots, goldfish, and cats from loneliness in similar ways. Why? That's just how the Swiss roll.

A list of the most popular names for the daughters of drummers

3. Anna One
2. Anna Two
1. Anna One Two Three Four

A list of fun words beginning with the letters Fl

8. Flummery
7. Flammulation
6. Flippity-floppity-floop
5. Flimflam
4. Flobbage
3. Flibbertigibbet
2. Flamdoodle
1. Flipfloppery (not in the dictionary, but it should be)

A list of music jokes

3. What do you call someone who hangs out with musicians?

   A drummer

2. What's the difference between a drummer and a vacuum cleaner?

   You have to plug one of them in before it sucks

1. What does a drummer use for contraception?

   His personality*

---

* In all seriousness, I have nothing against drummers (some of my best friends are drummers).

A list of expressions about chatterboxes from around the world

7. You could talk the hind legs off a donkey (UK)
6. You could talk the ears off a chicken (US)
5. You talk like a waterfall (Germany)
4. You talk like you've been hired (Poland)
3. You were born mouth first (Japan)
2. You give me blisters in the ears (Norway)
1. You twirl your tongue as the cow twirls its tail (Russia)

A list of words and phrases that are older than you think

8. Fangirl (1934)
7. OMG (1917)
6. Legit (1897)
5. Fake news (1890)
4. Xmas (1755)
3. Hubby (1682)
2. Newfangled (1496)
1. That chonky boi is swole and thicc (217 BC)

---

* The first known use of OMG comes from a letter to Winston Churchill (in 1917). And Churchill himself later used OMG in one of his famous speeches:

> "We shall fight on the beaches
>
> We shall fight on the landing grounds
>
> We shall fight in the fields and in the streets
>
> And they'll be all like omg just stop already wtf."

A list of my biggest flaws

10. Disturbingly obsessed with lists

9. Often repeat myself

7. Useless at counting

6. Always putting myself down

5. Terrible person

4. Often repeat myself

3. Weird toes

2. Never finish things

1.

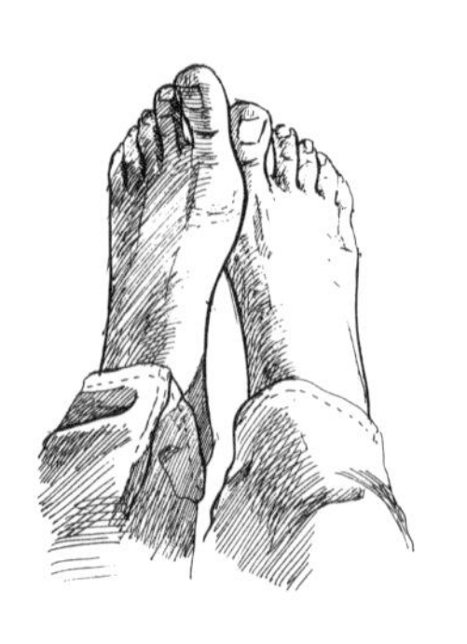

A list of things it's raining . . .

8. Cats and dogs (English)
7. Old ladies and sticks (Welsh)
6. Like a pissing cow (French)
5. As from Esteri's ass (Finnish)
4. Female trolls (Norwegian)
3. Chair legs (Greek)
2. Wheelbarrows (Czech)
1. Men (hallelujah)

A list of things I believed in childhood that may have been wrong

5. Everyone gets a turn at being Prime Minister
4. Fish fingers are actual fingers
3. The A in *The A-Team* stands for Adam
2. Teachers don't exist outside of school hours
1. In the old days, the whole world was black and white

A list of ways to express elation in different languages*

8. I'm on cloud nine (English)
7. I'm on the pig's back (Irish)
6. I have a face full of spring air (Mandarin)
5. I have a wedding party up my butt (Farsi)
4. I have the potato (French)
3. I'm in butter (Estonian)
2. I feel poodle-well (German)
1. I'm as happy as MacGyver in an ironmonger's (Spanish)

A bonus list of "Smiling from ear to ear" in different languages

3. Grinning like a Cheshire cat (English)
2. Grinning like a cooked head (Turkish)
1. Smiling like an idiot to his cheese (Polish)

---

* There's also a lovely expression for becoming overcome with joy in Hindi and Urdu—*Dil baagh baagh ho gaya*—which means "my heart became a garden."

A list of unnecessary, needless, and gratuitous tautologies

7. Shrugged his shoulders (what else would he shrug?)

6. Nodded her head (see above)

5. ATM machine (see also PIN number)

4. Future plans (see also past experience)

3. Fiction novel (urgh)

2. Safe haven (urghhhhhh)

1. Revert back (unforgivable)

A list of people killed by fruits and vegetables

5. Frederick III, Holy Roman Emperor (melon overdose)
4. Comic poet Antiphanes (struck by a pear)
3. Stuntman Bobby Leach (slipped on an orange peel)
2. Health-food advocate Basil Brown (carrot juice poisoning)
1. English politician Sir William Payne-Gallwey (fell and landed on a turnip)

A list of how to say "Zero fucks given" throughout Europe

8. It bothers me like a cardboard duck (Denmark)
7. I don't give a cabbage (Italy)
6. It's sausage to me (Germany)
5. It hurts me in the lighthouse (Bulgaria)
4. It interests me as much as a kilogram of shit (Finland)
3. I slap my balls on it (France)
2. It can oxidize on my anus (the Netherlands)
1. Flowers on my dick and bees all around (Greece)

A list of films that sound rude but aren't

10. *Deep Impact*
9. *The Bone Collector*
8. *Fists of Fury*
7. *Fire Down Below*
6. *Let the Right One In*
5. *The Harder They Come*
4. *Feeling Minnesota*
3. *Failure to Launch*
2. *Inside Llewyn Davis*
1. *Big*

A list of outdated English slang for being intoxicated

7. Full to the bowtie (1959)
6. Whittled as a penguin (1906)
5. Plum full of bug juice (1894)
4. Malty (1811)
3. Coming home by the villages (1770)
2. Drunk as a wheelbarrow (1675)
1. Bumpsy (1611)

A list of outdated English slang for a hangover

8. Cocktail flu (2004)
7. Mouth like the bottom of a birdcage (1944)
6. The woofits (1918)
5. The miserables (1902)
4. Feeling like a stewed owl (1892)
3. Barrel fever (1878)
2. The jim-jams (1852)
1. The horrors (1791)

A bonus list of names for a hangover from different languages

5. A monkey (Slovak)
4. A howling of kittens (Polish)
3. Carpenters in the head (Danish)
2. A wooden mouth (French)
1. Next-day-ishness (Hungarian)

A list of classic George W. Bush quotes (Bushisms)

5. Families is where our nation finds hope, where wings take dream
4. I think we agree, the past is over
3. I know how hard it is for you to put food on your family
2. One of the great things about books is sometimes there are some fantastic pictures
1. Rarely is the question asked: Is our children learning?

A list of savage curses from around the world

8. May a goose kick you (Poland)
7. May your VCR catch fire (Greece)
6. May your future child be born without a butthole (China)
5. May your obituary be written in weasel's piss (Ireland)
4. May you be fucked by a wheelbarrow full of small monkeys (Hungary)
3. May your mother-in-law's curry get burnt (Gujarat)
2. May your wife give birth to a centipede so you spend your life working for shoes (Serbia)
1. Let it be the will of god that you shit yourself (Bosnia)

A bonus list of the most merciless of them all, the Slovenian curses (not for the fainthearted)

3. May your kale rot
2. May the hen kick you
1. I hope your tractor breaks

A list of countries by number of tractors per 10,000 people

7. Philippines (1)
6. Croatia (5)
5. China (7)
4. India (14)
3. South Africa (16)
2. Mexico (18)
1. Slovenia (574)

A list of contemporary curses for your worst enemy

8. May all your snacks be really healthy

7. May your bare feet always find a Lego

6. May you forever put your USB in upside down

5. May you have more clothes than hangers

4. May all your favorite bands get into saxophone solos

3. May the cheese on your nachos be unevenly distributed

2. May neither side of your pillow be cool

1. May your country of origin never be the first option in the drop-down box

A list of "It's a piece of cake" in different languages

5. It's a little egg (Dutch)
4. It's a roll with butter (Polish)
3. It's papaya with sugar (Portuguese)
2. It's as simple as beans (Hungarian)
1. It's an easy wiener (Finnish)

A list of films to watch in winter

8. *Scarf-face*
7. *Casablanket*
6. *Jurassic Parka*
5. *Fleece Academy*
4. *Thermals and Louise*
3. *The Men Who Stare at Coats*
2. *What's Heating Gilbert Grape*
1. *The Good, the Bad and the Snuggly*

A bonus list of books to read in winter

5. *The Importance of Being Furnaced*
4. *Snow Country for Cold Men*
3. *A Farewell to (Bare) Arms*
2. *Catch Twenty-flu*
1. *The Chilliad*

A list of names for jellyfish from different languages

7. Sea glitter (Icelandic)
6. Moon of the sea (Japanese)
5. Bride of the sea (Persian)
4. Wibbly wobbly fish (Welsh slang)
3. Seal snot (Irish)
2. Bad water (Peruvian Spanish)
1. Whale vomit (Faroese)*

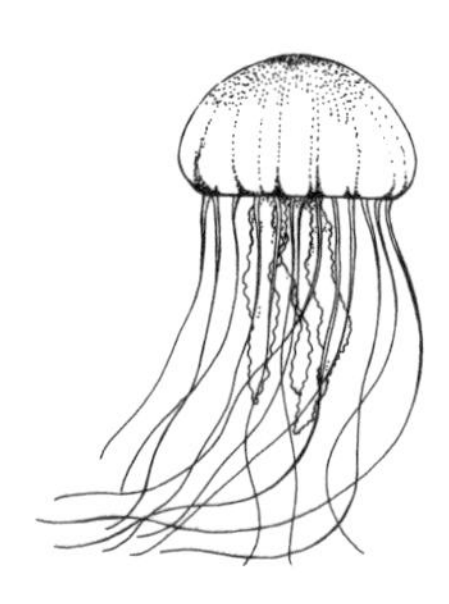

---

* Honorable mention to Danish, which has several great words for jellyfish. If it's a non-stinging jellyfish, it's called *vandman,* which translates to "waterman." A stinging jellyfish is called brandman or "fire man." And then there's the general term *gople,* which derives from the Norwegian dialectical *gopla,* which essentially means "mass of slime."

A list of my least favorite twentieth-century colloquialisms

8. Booyah
7. Gnarly
6. Goober
5. . . . Not!
4. As if
3. Psych!
2. Take a chill pill
1. Party-hardy

A list of words most often spelled wrong*

7. Accomodate
6. Dilemna
5. Embarass
4. Jewelery
3. Seperate
2. Mischievious
1. Wrong

---

* Here, in case you're interested, is a poem I wrote on the subject:

EVIL MISS PELLINGS

Miss Pellings can come at any thyme
Especially when you're trying to rime

She's hear and their and everywear
With clause as sharp as grizzly bare

It's quiet likely that you'll see her
In rythm, scism, onomatopeaia

You may think she's gone, breathe a sigh of relief
But no, here she is, back to cause you more greif

—Addam Sharpe

A list of useful Swedish words

5. *Skitstövel* (a douchebag, literally "shit boot")
4. *Knullruffs* (messy hair after sleeping with someone, literally "fuck hair")
3. *Sliddersladder* (a gossip)
2. *Slutspurt* (a clearance sale, literally "race to the end")
1. *Snuskhummer* (a pervert, literally "filthy-minded lobster")*

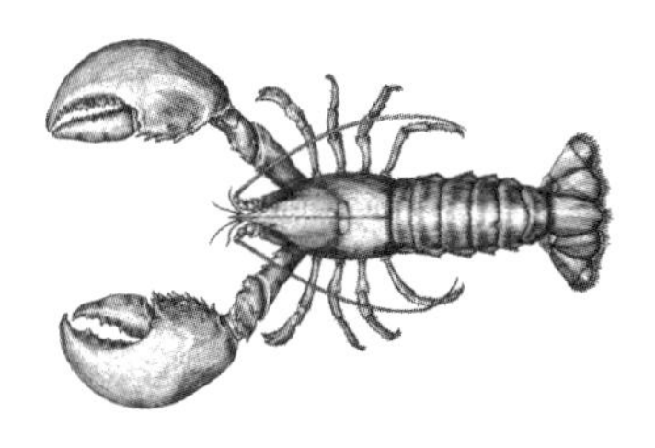

---

* Another great Swedish word was *ogooglebar* (someone, or something, that doesn't show up in an online search, literally "ungoogleable"), but sadly the Language Council of Sweden decided to drop it from its list of new words after legal pressure from Google.

A list of fun alternatives for existing words

8. Disco chicken (peacock)
7. Food library (fridge)
6. Berry fucker (blender)
5. Milk racist (lactose intolerant)
4. Prison donkey (zebra)
3. City boner (skyscraper)
2. Anger parade (protest)
1. American murder log (alligator)

A list of useful Australian phrases*

7. My mouth's drier than a dead dingo's donger (I'm thirsty)
6. I could eat the crutch out of a low-flying duck (I'm hungry)
5. I'm as full as a doctor's wallet (I'm no longer hungry)
4. Don't come the raw prawn (don't try to fool me)
3. She has a few kangaroos loose in the top paddock (she's crazy)
2. He has a face like a dropped pie (he's unattractive)
1. I'm not here to fuck spiders (I'm not messing around)

---

* Bonus Australian fact: An episode of the British show *Peppa Pig* has twice been pulled off air in Australia after being deemed inappropriate for Aussie children. The episode's main message was "spiders can't hurt you."

A list of organisms by number of chromosomes

8. Fruit fly (8)
7. Housefly (12)
6. Frog (26)
5. Fox (34)
4. Cat (38)
3. Dolphin (44)
2. Human (46)
1. Pineapple (50)*

* I, for one, welcome our future pineapple overlords.

A list of euphemisms for being on your period from different languages

7. It's strawberry week (German)
6. It's lingonberry week (Swedish)
5. The English have landed (French)
4. The Russians have arrived (Romanian)
3. Japan is attacking (Finnish)
2. Santa Claus has come (Hungarian)
1. There are communists in the funhouse (Danish)

A list of names for book clubs

10. Page Against the Machine
9. Painfully Shelf Aware
8. Cool Story Poe
7. Candide Discussions
6. The Plath to Enlightenment
5. It's a Hardback Life
4. We Like Big Books and We Cannot Lie
3. Orwell-endowed
2. Philip K. Dick Picks
1. Prose Before Hoes

A list of names for love handles from different languages

3. Fuck reins (Flemish)
2. Little breads (Greek)
1. Hip gold (German)

A bonus list of names for a tummy paunch

3. The three folds of wisdom (French)*
2. A company director's stomach (Japanese)
1. A cemetery for fried chickens (Austrian German)

---

* The German "hip gold" and French "three folds of wisdom" sound almost flattering, like something you might find on a Valentine's card:

> Roses are red
> Hips are gold
> You have so much wisdom
> It's at least threefold

A list of writing tips

5. Never use a big word when a Lilliputian one will do

4. If you want your writing to be accessible and modern, avoid euphuistic and erstwhile parlance

3. Don't use obsolete words, or you may jargogle your reader

2. You shouldn't clutter your prose with tautologies, pleonasms, or superfluousness

1. And never, under any circumstances, begin a sentence with AND. Or any other conjunction. Unless you want to

A list of the most satisfying words to say aloud

8. Discombobulation
7. Higgledy-piggledy
6. Zamboni
5. Nincompoop
4. Mellifluous
3. Flump
2. Pumpernickel
1. I told you so

A bonus list of the most satisfying names to say aloud

5. Kublai Khan
4. Bam Bam Bigelow
3. Evonne Goolagong
2. Boutros Boutros-Ghali
1. Engelbert Humperdinck

A list of whatchamacallits in different languages

7. Thingamajig (English)
6. *Chingadera* (Mexican Spanish)*
5. *Himstergims* (Danish)†
4. *Naninani* (Japanese)‡
3. *Zamazingo* (Turkish)
2. *Dingsbums* (German)
1. *Huppeldepup* (Dutch)§

---

* *Chingadera* is very much an adult version of thingamajig—it basically translates to "the fucking thing"—so be careful using it in polite company.

† The Danish word *himstergims* is usually spelled *himstregims*, but I went with the rarer spelling because it evokes the image of an Olympic Games . . . but for hamsters.

‡ The Japanese word *naninani* essentially means the "what-what."

§ The most common Dutch word for thingamajig is *dinges*. Some Dutch people do use *huppeldepup* for thingamajig, but it more often refers to an unknown person (a whatshisname). I used it anyway though. Because how could I not? *Huppeldepup!*

A list of the most difficult words to say aloud

8. Specificity
7. Ignominious
6. Library
5. Defibrillator
4. Worcestershire
3. Pulchritude
2. Asterisk
1. Sorry*

---

* Seems to be the hardest word.

A list of how to say "The pot calling the kettle black" around the world

5. The owl calls the sparrow big-headed (Hungary)
4. The hospital mocks charity (France)
3. The armadillo says the turtle is too hard-shelled (Venezuela)
2. The dirty one badmouths the badly washed (Brazil)
1. The eye mucus laughs at the nose dirt (Japan)

A list of anagrams

10. Elvis (lives!)
9. Halley's Comet (shall yet come)
8. Princess Diana (end is a car spin)
7. Sycophant (acts phony)
6. President Clinton of the USA
   (to copulate, he finds interns)
5. Editor (redo it)
4. Father-in-law (near halfwit)
3. Feeling romantic (flaming erection)
2. Admirer (married)
1. Procrastination (satanic porn riot)

A list of the most fearsome national animals

7. Brown bear (Russia)
6. Bull (Spain)
5. Wolf (Estonia)
4. Leopard (Rwanda)
3. Black panther (Gabon)
2. Bengal tiger (India)
1. Unicorn (Scotland)

A list of my thoughts on beginning correspondence with "Dear Sirs or Madams"

3. Dull

2. Binary

1. What is this, the 1800s?

A list of why beginning correspondence with "Dear Gentlebeings" is better

3. Pizzazzy

2. Inclusive

1. Hints that you may be a superior (but friendly) alien life-form

A list of great movie taglines

7. Escape or die frying (*Chicken Run*)
6. Just deux it (*Hot Shots! Part Deux*)
5. Yippee-ki-yay Mother Russia (*A Good Day to Die Hard*)
4. The wait is ogre (*Shrek the Third*)
3. Family isn't a word. It's a sentence (*The Royal Tenenbaums*)
2. The longer you wait, the harder it gets (*The 40-Year-Old Virgin*)
1. Unwittingly, he trained a dolphin to kill the president of the United States (*The Day of the Dolphin*)

A list of "Costs an arm and a leg" expressed in different languages

5. Costs an eye from the head (Italian)
4. Costs a rib from the body (Dutch)
3. Costs the shirt and the pants (Norwegian)
2. Costs as much as St. Peter paid for his scrambled eggs (Serbo-Croatian)
1. It's pig expensive (German)

A bonus list of ways to say "Dirt cheap" in different languages

5. Cheap as a banana (Portuguese)
4. Cheaper than radishes (Arabic)
3. Cheaper than a mushroom (Lithuanian)
2. I bought it for an apple and an egg (Dutch)
1. It's pig cheap (Norwegian)

A list of names for fan groups

7. Pine-Nuts (Chris Pine)
6. Cumberbitches (Benedict Cumberbatch)
5. Liv Laugh Lovers (Liv Tyler)
4. McAvoyeurs (James McAvoy)
3. Degenerates (Ellen DeGeneres)
2. Goulddiggers (Ellie Goulding)
1. Di-Hards (Princess Diana)

A list of reasons Bono sucks

5. Egomaniac
4. Short-man complex
3. Stupid white tights
2. Always starting wars
1. Trounced at Waterloo (probably why he never takes off those sunglasses)*

---

* You may be thinking to yourself, "Erm, Adam, I think you're confusing Bono and Napoleon Bonaparte. You do realize they're different people, right?" To which I say, "Have you ever seen Bono and Bonaparte in the same room?" I rest my case!

A list of words improved in translation

7. Stapler = paper vampire (Afrikaans)
6. Cotton candy = daddy's beard (French)
5. Auction = shouting shop (Finnish)
4. Necktie = larynx loincloth (Hindi)
3. Diabetes = sugar piss disease (Thai)
2. Funeral = into-the-ground-ening (German)
1. Marriage = house prison (Burmese)

A bonus list of animal names improved in translation

5. Dolphin = sea pig (Japanese)
4. Penguin = fat goose (Icelandic)
3. Turkey = threatening chicken (German)*
2. Horse = supernatural dog (Sioux)
1. Tadpole = butt troll (Norwegian)

---

* The German word is *Truthahn. Hahn* is the chicken part (a rooster, more specifically). And there's some debate whether the word *trut* is just onomatopoeic (a *trut-trut-trut* sound turkeys might make) or whether it actually comes from the middle German *droten* (to threaten). I'm obviously in camp *droten* because "threatening chicken" rules.

A list of collective nouns for people

8. A coincidence?! of conspiracy theorists

7. An enlargement of pianists

6. An anarchy of librarians

5. A rash of dermatologists

4. A great deal of car salesmen

3. A lot of parking attendants

2. A fuckery of politicians

1. A sophistication of Kardashians

A list of absurd newspaper headlines, set to the "Roses Are Red" rhyme

5. Roses are red

   Life is a journey

   MAN ACCUSED OF KILLING LAWYER RECEIVES A NEW ATTORNEY

4. Roses are red

   Let's go to France

   MAN WITH NOTHING TO DECLARE HAD FIFTY-FIVE TORTOISES IN HIS PANTS

3. Roses are red

   Look out for felons

   FARMER USING CANNON TO PROTECT WATERMELONS

2. Roses are red

   Pink's for hydrangeas

   ONE-ARMED MAN APPLAUDS THE KINDNESS OF STRANGERS

1. Roses are red

   Wonders never cease

   HOMICIDE VICTIMS RARELY TALK TO POLICE

A list of alternative deadly sins

7. RaiSIN (just a rubbish grape)
6. MoccaSIN (snakes terrible, shoes worse)
5. Sleeping with your couSIN (very bad)
4. InSINcerity
3. SINgalongs (especially to Frank SINatra)
2. SINgle-use straws
1. Wearing socks with sandals

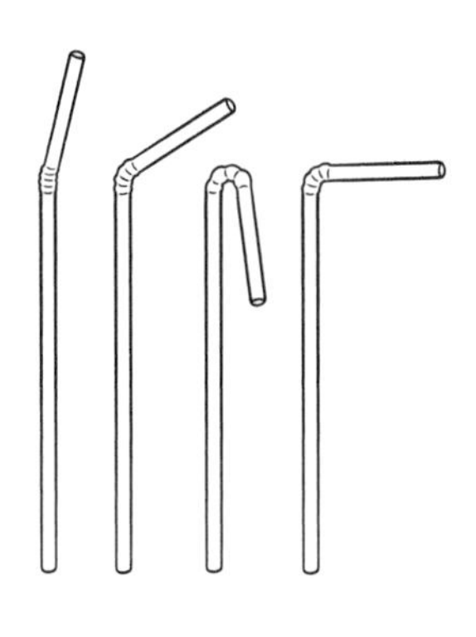

A list of my favorite types of lists

5. NoveLISTS
4. IdeaLISTS
3. UnicycLISTS
2. Good LISTeners
1. Top fives

A list of movie mash-ups I'd pay good money to see

7. *The Sixth Sense and Sensibility*

6. *Three Men and a Baby Driver*

5. *The Unbearable Lightness of Being John Malkovich*

4. *A Time to Kill a Mockingbird*

3. *Eat Pray Love in the Time of Cholera*

2. *A Passage to Indiana Jones and the Temple of Doom*

1. *Pumping Iron Man*

A list of useful Irish expressions

5. There's two gobshites in this town, and he's both of them
4. The pound would squeal before he'd let go of it
3. The tide wouldn't take her out
2. If there was work in the bed, he'd sleep on the floor
1. May the cat eat you and the devil eat the cat

A list of "I messed up" from different languages

7. I made a dog's dinner of it (British English)

6. I screwed the pooch (American English)

5. I fucked a hedgehog (Serbian)

4. There's pig's feet on me (Welsh)

3. I threw my boogers in the beans (Romanian)

2. I bundled it brown (Spanish)

1. I stirred the tea with my dick (Russian)

A list of helpful life advice

5. "Always be sincere, even when you don't mean it."

   —Irene Peter

4. "Always live within your income, even if you have to borrow to do so."

   —Josh Billings

3. "All generalizations are bad."

   —R. H. Grenier

2. "We must believe in free will. We have no choice."

   —Isaac Bashevis Singer

1. "Always go to other people's funerals; otherwise, they won't come to yours."

   —Yogi Berra

0. "Shoot for the moon, and if you miss, you will be among the stars, where there is no gravity or oxygen, and you will just float around out there, asphyxiating and alone. And then die."

   —Adam Sharp

A list of expressions for lazybones from different languages*

8. Lazy sock (German)
7. Lazyworm (Finnish)
6. Snake king (Cantonese)
5. Director of free air (Lithuanian)
4. A day thief (Flemish)
3. A nothing-doer (Hungarian)
2. A flaccid fish (Norwegian)
1. A sluggish banana (Danish)

---

* My favorite English word related to laziness is the sixteenth-century "lubberland" (a mythical place reserved for lazy people).

A list of importmanteaus (important + portmanteaus)

7. Floordrobe (floor + wardrobe)
6. Sneezure (sneeze + seizure)
5. Shituation (shit + situation)
4. Enormouse (enormous + mouse)
3. Drunkle (drunk + uncle)
2. Zombeavers (zombie + beavers)
1. Merverts (mermaids + perverts)*

---

* Something really needs to be done about those damn merverts!

A list of film title translations from around the world

5. *The Terminator = The Electronic Murderer* (Poland)
4. *The Waterboy = Dimwit Surges Forth* (Thailand)
3. *The Full Monty = Six Naked Pigs* (China)
2. *Leaving Las Vegas = I'm Drunk, and You're a Prostitute* (Japan)
1. *Dragnet = Floppy Coppers Don't Bite* (Germany)

A bonus list of TV show title translations from around the world

5. *Six Feet Under = The Customer Is Always Dead* (Russia)
4. *Big Bang Theory = Spectacles Fogged Up* (Finland)
3. *Breaking Bad = Total Suckage* (Hungary)
2. *The Fresh Prince of Bel-Air = A Crazy in the Hood* (Brazil)
1. *Jersey Shore = Macaroni Rascals* (Japan)

A list of real people born to do their jobs*

8. Les McBurney (firefighter)
7. Sara Blizzard (weather presenter)
6. Rich White (Kentucky Republican)
5. Rachel B. Pullin (dentist)
4. John Bastard (British politician)
3. Sue Yoo (lawyer)
2. Marina Stepanova (hurdler)
1. Dick Chopp (vasectomy specialist)

---

* In 1940s and 1950s London, women were only allowed to appear nude on stage if they did not move. The senior censor who checked that such nudity rules were being upheld was named George Titman.

A list of expressions for simultaneous sun and rain around the world

5. Foxes are taking a bath (Finland)
4. A poor man got rich (Kazakhstan)
3. Witches are combing their hair (Catalonia)
2. The devil is making pancakes (Oldenburg)
1. A zombie is beating his wife for salty food (Haiti)

A list of collective nouns for books

8. A pretension of literary fiction
7. A range of mountaineering guides
6. A shroud of mysteries
5. A cumulation of wealth management textbooks
4. An exaggeration of autobiographies
3. A sshh-load of library books
2. A hoard of erotica
1. Too many cookbooks

A list of club rules

5. First rule of Polite Club:

   Please don't talk about Polite Club.
   Many thanks in advance, and enjoy the rest of your day.

4. First rule of Gaslight Club:

   Let's not talk about Gaslight Club.
   You'll only get upset again.

3. First rule of Rewrite Club:

   ~~Do not talk about~~ Don't discuss Rewrite Club.

2. First rule of Garrulous Club:

   Do not—actually, speaking of rules, funny story: I was at a bar last week when my friend Pete walked in—do you know Pete? Funny thing about Pete, he once went on vacation to Barbados for two weeks, or was it three weeks? Hang on, it'll come to me. Actually, it was ten days . . .

1. First rule of Suspense Club:

A list of euphemisms that really get on my you-know-whats

7. Non-traditional shopper (looter)
6. Alternative dentation (false teeth)
5. Netflix expert (unemployed)
4. Health-alteration specialist (assassin)
3. Bad luck when it comes to thinking (stupid)
2. Expeditious driving award (speeding ticket)
1. Living impaired (dead)

A bonus list of euphemisms about dying from around the world

5. Put aside your clogs (Denmark)
4. Throw out your best skates (Russia)
3. Hang your tennis shoes (Mexico)
2. Go to the land of no hats (Haiti)
1. Go take your free kick at Hitler's backside (my granddad's house)

A list of my dream jobs

8. Waterslide tester

7. Professional cuddler

6. Private island caretaker

5. Panda nanny

4. Minding my own business

3. Releaser of the hounds

2. Crusher of enemies

1. Head of potatoes

A list of reasons to love Finland

5. When you finish your Finnish PhD, you get a top hat and a sword
4. There's a Burger King in Helsinki that has a sauna
3. Mobile phone–throwing is a national sport
2. There's an annual day for celebrating failure
1. The Finnish word *Juoksentelisinkohan* means, "I wonder if I should run around aimlessly?"

A list of unusual fears

8. Lutraphobia (otters)
7. Nomophobia (no mobile phone reception)
6. Gowiththeflowbia (easygoingness)
5. Hippopotomonstrosesquipedaliophobia (long words)
4. Aibohphobia (palindromes)
3. Ragmanaphobia (anagrams)
2. Baracknophobia (Obama)
1. Twitophobia (reaching character limit bef

A list of "Beating around the bush" in different languages

5. Circling the almond (Maltese)
4. Getting the partridge dizzy (Spanish)
3. Doing the egg dance (German)
2. Giving birth to a calf (Russian)
1. Prancing like a cat around hot porridge (Finnish)

A list of alternatives to the name Benedict Cumberbatch

7. Buckminster Chowderpants
6. Bentobox Crumplehorn
5. Bumpersticker Cogglesnatch
4. Bongobopper Toodlesnoot
3. Tumbledaddy Gibbygobbler
2. Thunderbeaver Skuzzledink
1. Billyray Snickersbar

A list of classic malaphors*

8. Love is a dish best served cold
7. It's not rocket surgery
6. We'll burn that bridge when we get to it
5. People in glass houses shouldn't dance like nobody's watching
4. Desperate times come to those who wait
3. If you want something done right, you're part of the problem
2. Money doesn't fall far from the tree
1. Whatever doesn't kill you will try, try again

A bonus list of classic malapropisms†

5. Stop looking for escape goat
4. You're always going off on a tandem
3. Patience is a virgin
2. You look like Jeff warmed up
1. I deserve proper constipation for my work

---

* A malaphor is when two figures of speech (idioms, clichés, aphorisms, etc.) get mixed together.

† A malapropism is when one word in a figure of speech is mistaken for another, similar-sounding word.

A list of alternatives to "When pigs fly" in different countries*

7. When donkeys fly (Italy)
6. When tractors will fall (Slovakia)
5. When monkeys fly out of my butt (Canada)†
4. When hens have teeth (France)
3. When the pig in yellow slippers climbs the pear tree (Bulgaria)
2. When cats grow horns (Indonesia)
1. When the 7-Eleven closes (Thailand)

---

* My absolute favorite is, "That'll happen when the garden is full of ducks, holding pastry in their hands," from a book claiming it to be Turkish. However, I asked many Turkish speakers, and not one had ever heard of it (which is why it sadly didn't make the list). With sayings like this, there are often many variants from each country, and I'm not usually interested in listing the most common or current. In fact, my favorites are the obscure ones, known only to specific generations or regions. But nevertheless, I do always insist on finding at least two native speakers who know the phrase before including it.

† The Canadian phrase is more specifically from *Wayne's World*, starring Canadian comedian Mike Myers.

A list of the worst trends in history

8. Fidget spinners
7. Planking
6. Magic Eye pictures (because I could never do them)
5. Candy Crush (because of the eight million daily invites)
4. Keep Calm memes
3. Flowers in beards
2. Man buns
1. Burning witches

A bonus list of the best trends in history

5. *Snake* on Nokia
4. Push Pops
3. Garbage Pail Kids
2. Myspace
1. Books of lists

A list of historical figures and their feelings toward cats

7. Abraham Lincoln (lover)
6. Mussolini (hater)
5. Anne Frank (lover)
4. Genghis Khan (hater)
3. Florence Nightingale (lover)
2. Ivan the Terrible (hater)
1. Erwin Schrödinger (undecided)

A list of delightful middle names

8. Delight (Quincy Jones)
7. Hercules (Elton John)
6. Shrader (Jennifer Lawrence)
5. John Mungo (Hugh Grant)
4. Bass (Courteney Cox)
3. Gerard (Mike Tyson)
2. Tiffany (Richard Gere)
1. Macauley Culkin (Macauley Culkin)*

---

* Macauley Culkin's actual middle name is Carson, but he asked his fans on Twitter what he should change it to and promised to legally adopt their choice. They decided he should be called Macauley Macauley Culkin Culkin, which actually shows quite a lot of restraint. I, for example, would have gone with one of these:

5. Macauley Sulkin Culkin
4. Macauley Loves-Giblets Culkin
3. Macauley Forever-Home-Alone Culkin
2. Macauley Wets-the-Bed Culkin
1. Macauley This-Is-a-Desperate-Cry-for-Help Culkin

A list of surplus middle name facts

3. You may think Michael J. Fox's middle name begins with a J, but actually, he just went with that letter because it sounds cool (his middle name is, in fact, Andrew)

2. The reason T. S. Eliot insisted that his middle initial always be used was because he was all too aware of what T. Eliot spelled backward

1. My middle initial is C, which is THE only thing about my extremely embarrassing middle name I'll ever reveal. So there!

A list of "Like a fish out of water" in different languages

7. Like an elf outside a hill (Icelandic)
6. Like a dog at a game of cones (Danish)
5. Like a Dane on skis (Norwegian)
4. Like a jackdaw among peacocks (Irish)
3. Like a cockroach at a chicken dance (Venezuelan Spanish)
2. Like a frog in a bowl of punch (Croatian)
1. Like an octopus in a garage (Spanish)

A list of film titles that contain spoilers

5. *Saving Private Ryan*
4. *Death of a Salesman*
3. *Free Willy*
2. *Lone Survivor*
1. *The Assassination of Jesse James by the Coward Robert Ford*

A list of famous books with fruit in the title

8. *A Clockwork Orange*
7. *The House on Mango Street*
6. *The Grapes of Wrath*
5. *War and Peach*
4. *Lime and Plumishmen*t
3. *The Girl with the Dragon Fruit Tattoo*
2. *The Berry Hungry Caterpillar*
1. *The Chronicles of Banania*

A list of how to say "All talk and no action" around the world

5. All hat and no cattle (Texas)
4. All noise and few walnuts (Spain)
3. A lot of foam and not much chocolate (Dominican Republic)
2. The thunder is loud, but the rain is light (China)
1. If he made one hundred knives, none would have a handle (Iran)

---

* *Mucho Ruido y Pocas Nueces (All Noise and Few Walnuts)* is also the Spanish title of Shakespeare's *Much Ado About Nothing*.

A list of pet names inspired by famous people

8. Chairman Meow (cat)

7. Bark Obama (dog)

6. Piggie Smalls (mini pig)

5. Kevin Bacon (regular pig)

4. Gregory Peck (hen)

3. Hennifer Lopez (rooster)

2. Chameleo Estevez (chameleon)

1. Al Capony (horse)

A list of my favorite international idioms

7. Like a crocodile in a wallet factory (Puerto Rican Spanish for nervous)

6. Not my circus, not my monkeys (Polish for not my problem)

5. You're scratching a lion's balls with a short stick (Afrikaans for pushing your luck)

4. He slid in on a shrimp sandwich (Swedish for being privileged)

3. That's the beans that fell on me (Bosnian for that's the way the cookie crumbles)

2. Life is not a pony farm (German for life is hard)

1. You work less than Tarzan's tailor (Spanish for lazy)

A list of my thoughts about "liking" a post on social media

3. Boring

2. Weak

1. Everyone does it

A list of why replying with "this pleases me" is better

3. Enigmatic

2. Suggests people should curry favor with you

1. It's what Benedict Cumberbatch would do

A list of "It's all Greek to me" in different languages

7. This is a Spanish village to me (Czech)
6. This is a Czech movie (Polish)
5. I don't grasp a bean (Danish)
4. It looks like fried calabash fritters (Burmese)
3. Is this ghost script? (Cantonese)
2. I can't make any chocolate from that (Dutch)
1. I only understand "train station" (German)

A list of words Shakespeare invented

8. Braggartism
7. Hobnob
6. Bedazzled
5. Pedantical
4. Skimble-skamble
3. Swagger
2. New-fangled
1. Plumpy

A bonus list of Shakespearean insults

5. Thine face is not worth sunburning
4. Your brain is as dry as the remainder biscuit after voyage
3. Away, you three-inch fool!
2. You, minion, are too saucy
1. I do desire that we may be better strangers

A list of what syphilis was originally called in different countries

7. The Italian Disease (France)
6. The French Disease (Italy)
5. The British Disease (Tahiti)
4. The Polish Disease (Russia)
3. The German Disease (Poland)
2. The Spanish Disease (the Netherlands)
1. The Chinese Pox (Japan)

A list of how to say "Nobody asked you!" around the world

8. Mind your own beeswax (English)
7. Deal with your own onions (French)
6. Not your pigs, not your beans (Lithuanian)
5. Keep your own owl straight (Punjabi)
4. That porridge wasn't made for you (Zulu)
3. You have no camel in the caravan (Arabic)
2. Who gave you a candle for this vigil? (Spanish)
1. You're not getting fucked, so don't wiggle your ass (Russian)*

---

* While studying words and idioms from around the world, I've found that the Russian phrases are often the most vulgar (which is why the Russian language is one of my favorites). To give another example, there is a Russian phrase for when you're doing nothing/just wasting time that translates to "I'm kicking dicks."

A list of reasons why dolphins are total badasses

5. They chew on toxic puffer fish to get high
4. They can kill sharks with their noses
3. They love admiring themselves in mirrors
2. They enjoy orgies and go on killing sprees when sexually frustrated
1. They refuse to stand for national anthems*

* Dolphins are also incredibly intelligent. So intelligent that within a week of being in captivity, they can train people to stand on the very edge of the pool and throw them fish.

A list of words recently added to the Oxford English Dictionary

8. Sprogged (to have kids)
7. Bogosity (the quality of being bogus)
6. Cock-a-doodle-doing (boastful)
5. Awesomesauce (excellent)
4. Back-sass (to reply in a cheeky manner)
3. Gee-whizzery (excessive naivety)
2. Brewstered (rich)
1. Jerkface (an obnoxious person)

A list of "In the middle of nowhere" in different languages

7. Godforsaken-Place-upon-Perche (French)
6. On Lars Leaky-Butt's field (Danish)
5. In the house of the penis (Brazilian Portuguese)
4. Where the devil lost his underwear (Venezuelan Spanish)
3. Where birds won't shit (Mandarin)
2. Where dogs bark with their asses (Polish)
1. Where wolves fuck (Serbian)

A list of useful old words

8. Poop-noddy (a fool)
7. Fribbler (a commitment-phobe)
6. Gongoozle (to stare at a canal)
5. Beazled (exhausted)
4. Jingle-boy (a rich man)
3. Vampirarchy (like the patriarchy, but with vampires)
2. Gong-hole (toilet)
1. Unbepissed (not yet soaked with urine)

A list of ways to say "Sleeping like a baby" around the world

7. Sleeping like a rose (the Netherlands)
6. Sleeping like a fur coat (Hungary)
5. Sleeping like a gopher (Poland)
4. Sleeping like a cannon (Croatia)
3. Sleeping like a suitcase in the station (Romania)
2. Sleeping like a killed man (Russia)
1. Fast asleep with hands full of pancakes (Berkshire, United Kingdom)*

---

* And after a long sleep comes what, in eighteenth-century Scots, was referred to as "hurkle-durkling" (the act of lying around in bed long after you should have gotten up).

A list of slang for having sex through history

8. Netflix and chill (2009)
7. Play Mr. Wobbly hides his helmet (1996)
6. Arrive at the end of the sentimental journey (1896)
5. Do a bit of giblet pie (1892)
4. Dance the blanket hornpipe (1823)
3. Give one's arse a salad (1661)
2. Grope for trout in a peculiar river (1603)
1. Fuck (1508)

A multitudinous agglomeration of Pantagruelian words that beguile with their splendiferousness

7. Boondoggle
6. Braggadocio
5. Slangwhanger
4. Knickknackatory
3. Spaghettification
2. Adventuresomeness
1. Hemidemisemiquaver (should be said aloud, fast)

---

* Slangwhanger (a loud, abusive speaker or offensive writer) goes particularly well with another favorite of mine, slubberdegullion (a worthless wretch). For example . . . "You're a slangwhanging slubberdegullion, and I'm sick and tired of your skulduggery."

A list of what the platypus is called in different languages

5. Odd beak (Croatian)
4. Fat lips (Woiwurrung)
3. Broad nose (Icelandic)
2. Water mole (Arabic)
1. Duck mouth beast (Mandarin)

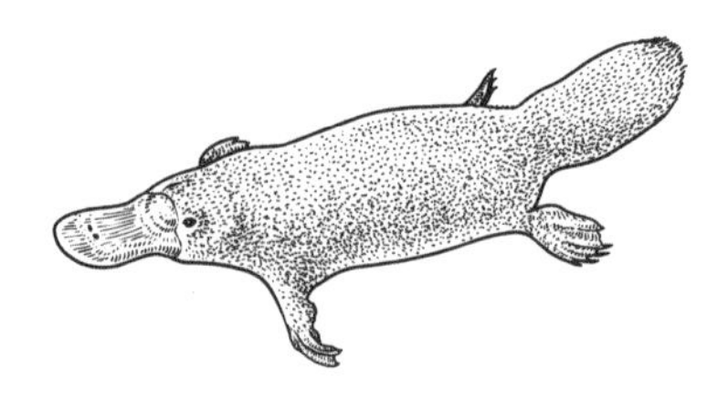

A list of the loudness of things in decibels

8. Refrigerator hum (40)
7. Vacuum (70)
6. Motorbike (90)
5. Police siren (120)
4. Plane taking off (140)
3. Shotgun blast (160)
2. Saturn V rocket launch (210)
1. Someone eating popcorn during a film (5,000)

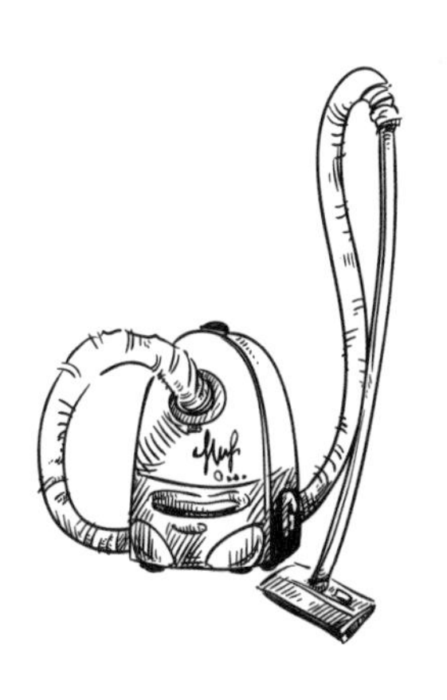

A list of international terms for the practice of each person covering their own expenses at a restaurant

5. Going Dutch (England)

4. English style (Egypt)

3. American style (Mexico)

2. Pay the bill the German way (Turkey)

1. By the law of Christ, each one with his own stew (Guatemala)

A list of types of exercise I try to avoid

7. Running my mouth

6. Jumping to conclusions

5. Pushing my luck

4. Kicking up a fuss

3. Skating on thin ice

2. Dancing with death

1. Swimming with the fishes

A list of types of drunk according to scientists*

5. The Hemingway (personality does not change)
4. The Mary Poppins (becomes much happier)
3. The Nutty Professor (becomes more social)
2. The Mr. Hyde (becomes more hostile)
1. The Ozzy Osbourne (becomes completely incoherent)†

---

* Interesting fact about drunkenness—in ancient Persia, all important debates took place with everyone drunk and then again with everyone sober, or vice versa, because an idea wasn't considered credible unless it sounded good in both states.

† I should mention that I made the last one up (and I'm no scientist).

A list of forgotten slang for body parts

8. Potato trap (mouth)
7. Idea pot (head)
6. Grabbing irons (fingers)
5. Prayer-bones (kneecaps)
4. Pudding-house (stomach)
3. Gooseberry grinder (bottom)
2. Matrimonial peacemaker (penis)
1. Cupid's kettle drums (breasts)

A list of spoonerisms

5. Cop porn (popcorn)
4. Don't pet the sweaty things (don't sweat the petty things)
3. Bully fooked (fully booked)
2. Bad salad (sad ballad)
1. Lack of pies (pack of lies)*

---

* I had another good one, but such is my hatred of top sixes that I decided I'd rather a five listing (or live fisting). But in case you were wondering, it was the name of a furniture showroom in New Zealand: Shack of Sit.

A list of international names for the @ symbol

8. Alpha twirl (Norwegian)
7. Strudel (Hebrew)
6. Cinnamon roll (Swedish)
5. Little duck (Greek)
4. Monkey bracket (German)
3. Meow sign (Finnish)
2. Moon's ear (Kazakh)
1. The "at" symbol (English, the language of Shakespeare)

A bonus list of old words for the exclamation mark (to show the English language can be inventive when it wants to be!)

5. Shriek-mark!
4. Wham!
3. Screech!
2. Dog's dick!
1. Shout-pole!

A list of oxymorons*

7. Pretty ugly
6. Fairly unjust
5. Kind of mean
4. Charm offensive
3. Microsoft Works
2. Government intelligence
1. Fun run

A bonus list of politically incorrect oxymorons that I've heard (but would never repeat!)

5. Quiet American
4. English cuisine
3. French Resistance
2. Secret vegan
1. Happily married

---

* The Chinese word for oxymoron, 矛盾語, means "spear and shield word" and refers to a story of a weapons merchant who claimed he had both shields no spear could pierce and spears which could pierce anything.

A list of proposed new meanings for existing words

10. Minimum (a tiny mother)
9. Out of bounds (an exhausted kangaroo)
8. Indispose (explaining how you want someone to stand)
7. Kidnapping (a sleeping child)
6. Arresting officer (a sleeping cop)
5. Whisky (a bit like a whisk)
4. Willy-nilly (impotent)
3. Avoidable (what a matador tries to do)
2. Heroes (what a guy in a boat does)
1. Coward (in the direction of a cow)

A list of PETA-approved idioms

8. Don't be so fig-headed
7. Like a broth to a flame
6. Sent on a wild juice chase
5. A leotard can't change its spots
4. Like a yam to the slaughter
3. Not enough room to swing a cactus
2. The world is your toaster
1. Hung like a horseradish

A list of variants of "A few sandwiches short of a picnic" around the world

5. She has mambo in the head (Argentina)
4. It's splashing on his lighthouse (Czech Republic)
3. Cows have drunk her brain (Croatia)
2. He doesn't have all the Moomins in the valley (Finland)
1. The wheel is spinning, but the hamster is dead (Sweden)

A bonus list of English variants of "A few sandwiches short of a picnic"

3. A few clowns short of a circus
2. A few tacos short of a combo plate
1. A few penguins short of a lawnmower

A list of the worst types of lists

8. Shopping lists (lead to shopping)
7. To-do lists (lead to having to do things)
6. Clickbait lists (number one will blow your mind!!!)
5. Colonialists (bad)
4. Top-four lists (evil)
3. Longlists (too long)
2. Shortlists (too short)
1. Santa lists (too many clauses)

A list of names for ladybugs around the world

7. Voodoo bug (Korea)
6. Little shoemaker (Iran)
5. Bishy barnabee (Norfolk, England)
4. Crawl Paul (Burgenland, Austria)
3. Stinky little turtle (China)*
2. Reddish female thing (Basque Country)†
1. Stubby red cow (Wales)

---

* "Stinky little turtle" isn't the general term for a ladybug but rather describes a specific type (one that emits a strange smell) found in certain parts of China. The standard name for a ladybug in Mandarin translates to "ladle bug."

† This is an etymological translation for the common word for ladybug in Basque—*marigorringo*—where *mari* originally meant "something female," and *gorringo* meant "reddish color." They are also sometimes called *amona mantangorri*, which today would be understood to mean "red apron granny."

A list of phrases to be used in conjunction with Joe Biden's "Lying dog-faced pony soldier"

5. Go kiss a jellyfish, ya mutton-munchin' mime grabber
4. Laugh it up, ya Twizzler-chompin cake walker
3. You're hitchhikin' to Memphis without a bindle, ya tomato-stewed gindaloon
2. Take a ruby red look at this ninny-lovin' cobra man
1. Cram it in your nethers, ya jazz-jivin' gopher gobbler

A list of names for Victorian ailments

7. The collywobbles (upset tummy)

6. A queer cog (rotten tooth)

5. Dropsy (oedema)

4. Strangery (rupture)

3. A churchyard cough (one likely to be fatal)

2. Scrivener's palsy (writer's cramp)

1. The unpleasantness (nothing good)

A list of names things used to be called

10. Thomas Mapother, IV (Tom Cruise)
9. Joaquin Bottom (Joaquin Phoenix)
8. Relentless (Amazon)
7. DrivUrSelf (Hertz)
6. Elf-chokes (hiccups)*
5. Windfuckers (kestrels)
4. Arsefeet (penguins)
3. *The Lunch Bunch* (*The Breakfast Club*)
2. *Toyz in the Hood* (*Toy Story*)
1. *Something That Happened* (*Of Mice and Men*)

---

* Hiccups were called elf-chokes or *ælfsogoða* in Old English because it was believed that they were caused by elves (sounds plausible enough to me).

A list of medical treatments from the past

8. Vibrators (for hysteria)
7. Cannibalism (for muscle cramps)
6. Heroin (for coughs)
5. Crystal meth (for asthma)
4. Arsenic (for arthritis)
3. Snail slime (for sore throats)
2. Blood of fallen gladiators (for epilepsy)
1. Teetotalism (to prevent spontaneous combustion)

A list of countries with the number of heavy metal bands per one million people

7. China (0.1)
6. Jamaica (0.3)
5. Thailand (2)
4. Cuba (6.4)
3. Japan (11)
2. Russia (14)
1. Finland (532)

A list of the number of people killed annually by . . .

8. Roller coasters (4)
7. Sharks (6)
6. Vending machines (8)
5. Champagne corks (24)
4. Cows (37)
3. Hot dogs (77)
2. Pen lids (115)
1. Exaggerated statistics (2.7 billion)

A list of songs about sandwiches

5. "Supermodel Sandwich W/Cheese" (Terence Trent D'Arby)
4. "Purgatory Sandwich With Mustard" (Deliverance)
3. "Sandwich of Love" (The Mentors)
2. "Give Me Back My Sandwich" (Five Iron Frenzy)
1. "Sandwiches Are Beautiful" (Bob King)

A list of how to tell someone to get lost in different countries

8. Go fry some asparagus (Colombia)
7. Go ski into a spruce (Finland)
6. Go collect some ants (Hungary)
5. Go to the farm to catch butterflies (Russia)
4. Go mushrooming (Latvia)*
3. Go get fucked by a blind bear (Albania)
2. Go stick a boat up your ass with the oars out (Italy)
1. I said good day, sir (England)

---

* Easily the most savage insult of them all because mushrooms are, in my opinion, carved from Satan's asshole.

A comprehensive list of all the foods that are worse than mushrooms

10.

9.

8.

7.

6.

5.

4.

3.

2.

1.

A list of international alternatives to "Say cheese!" when taking someone's picture*

8. Kimchi! (South Korea)
7. Omelet! (Sweden)
6. Cabbage! (Bulgaria)
5. Pea soup! (Estonia)
4. Ant shit! (Germany)
3. Pineapples can't pee! (Brazil)
2. Pepsi! (Thailand)
1. Smile, please (Poland)

* "Cheese" is used for taking photographs because saying the word aloud makes the mouth form into a smile-like shape. In the nineteenth century, however, it was considered childish to smile in photographs. People, therefore, said "prunes," which makes the mouth taut, helping to maintain a serious expression.

A list of things you shouldn't be fooled by

5. Nigerian princes asking for your bank details
4. Fake friend requests
3. Pyramid schemes
2. Russian dating agencies
1. The rocks that she's got (she's still, she's still Jenny from the block)

A list of the greatest metal band names from around the world

7. Aggressive Snail Attack (Croatia)
6. Teddy Bear Autopsy (Czech Republic)
5. We Butter the Bread with Butter (Germany)
4. Depressed Mode (Finland)
3. Lobster Apocalypse (United States)*
2. Bathtub Shitter (Japan)
1. Destiny Potato (Serbia)

A bonus list of metal band names from Canada

5. Kittie
4. Strapping Young Lad
3. Sympathy
2. Cellphone
1. Jesus Loves Anal

---

* Honorable mention to Baltimore death metal band Hatebeak, whose lead singer is a parrot.

A list of colorful exclamations

8. Great bald-faced hornets!
7. By the hokey-pokey!
6. Fuck a duck!
5. What fresh hell is this?
4. Oh, buggery botch-wagons! (strictly for posh people)
3. Blow my buttons!
2. Holy horror!
1. Jesus Christ on a raft!

A list of descriptions that have actually appeared in tabloid newspapers*

7. The big-hearted pop tiddler (Prince)
6. The revered reptile (tortoise)
5. The step-climbing meat-puncher (Rocky)
4. The highly regarded breakfast drink (orange juice)
3. The tiny totalitarian (Kim Jong-il)
2. Entitled pork chop (Peppa Pig)
1. Psychotic airborne scumbags (seagulls)

---

* These are sometimes referred to as knobbly monsters—a descriptive phrase (often contrived) used to avoid repeating the name of a person, place, or object in an article.

A list of things that are bad luck around the world

8. Friday the seventeenth (Italy)
7. Tuesday the thirteenth (Greece)
6. Seeing someone carrying empty buckets (Russia)
5. Yo-yos (Syria)
4. Complimenting a baby (Serbia)*
3. Pointing at stars (Brazil)
2. Upside-down bread (France)
1. Skydiving without a parachute (all countries)†

---

* According to this old Serbian superstition, if you say anything nice to a baby, it will then be vulnerable to the evil eye. So, if you ever meet a Serbian baby, go ahead and remark how hideously ugly it is.

† Another interesting superstition (too long to include in this list) is from Zimbabwe. It states that if a member of your family is kidnapped by a mermaid, you must not shed a single tear (because then they will never be returned).

A list of famous book titles with added clickbait

5. *You Simply Won't Believe How Many Flew Over the Cuckoo's Nest*
4. *Fifty Mind-Blowing Shades of Grey (No. 7 Is EPIC)*
3. *You'll Flip When You See What Madame Bovary Looks Like Now*
2. *Every Single Year of Solitude, Definitively Ranked*
1. *Nobody Can Figure Out Where Waldo Is, and It's Driving Them CRAZY*

A list of German words that begin with K

7. *Krimskrams* (knick-knacks)
6. *Krawattenmuffel* (one who doesn't like wearing ties)
5. *Kummerspeck* (weight gained from comfort eating, literally "grief bacon")
4. *Kindergarten* (nursery school, literally "children garden")*
3. *Kugelgrippe* (pregnant, literally "potbelly flu")
2. *Krankenwagen* (ambulance, literally "sick person car")
1. *Kaputt* (broken)

---

* Here's a poem I wrote that includes the word Kinder:

ROUGH? PLOUGH THROUGH THOUGH

They say if wordplay makes you numb

Math puns make you number

And if you stretch out every limb

It will surely get you limber

But though your children may be kind

The German kids are *Kinder*

And eye rhymes can be wild

But these ones just bewilder

A list of misnomers

8. Cat burglar (not a cat)
7. Guinea pig (not a pig)
6. Naked mole rat (not a mole, not a rat, not naked)
5. Funny bone (not a bone, not funny)
4. White chocolate (not chocolate)
3. Lone Ranger (always with his sidekick)
2. *The NeverEnding Story* (ends)
1. Baby food (contains *zero* babies)

A list of ways to start a conversation with a cat around the world

7. *Pss-pss-pss* (England)
6. *Kiss-kiss-kiss* (Finland)
5. *Pish-pish-pish* (Iran)
4. *Mee-mee-mee* (Myanmar)
3. *Minou-minou-minou* (France)
2. *Ming-ming-ming* (Philippines)
1. What's new pussycat, whoa, oh whoa (Wales)

A list of puns for your viewing pleasure

8. I was up all night trying to think of the perfect pun. And then it dawned on me
7. It's hard to explain puns to kleptomaniacs. They always take things literally
6. It's also hard for people to take pictures of themselves in the shower. They often have selfie steam issues
5. I once saw an innuendo competition advertised in the paper. So I entered my wife
4. What's the difference between a well-dressed man and an exhausted dog? One wears a suit, the other just pants
3. Why do riot police always get to work early? To beat the morning crowds
2. Why do teenagers travel in groups of three or five? Because they can't even
1. What's the definition of a Freudian Slip? When you say one thing but mean a mother

A list of ways to say "Speak of the devil" in different countries

5. Speak of the donkey (Greece)
4. When you speak of the trolls, they stand in the entrance hall (Sweden)
3. Mention the lion, he eats you (Tunisia)
2. Remember the shit, here it is (Russia)
1. I wish I had said "a million pounds" (Egypt)

A list of things that can't be done simultaneously

7. Pinch your nose and say "hmm" for more than three seconds
6. Breathe and swallow
5. Hum and whistle
4. Have your cake and eat it
3. Watch *Forrest Gump* and not cry
2. Be in China and check Facebook
1. Be productive and have a Twitter*

---

* Please forgive the Twitter references, but this book would never have happened without it. I've always been a Luddite and barely used any social media until late 2018 when I decided to have a go at tweeting. The character limit had just been increased from 140 to 280, and this meant that, as long as I kept them short, I could fit a list into a single tweet. Somehow these became popular, and it has been a great source of joy to me that a solitary lifelong obsession has been so warmly received by the wonderful and witty people that follow me (and who regularly contribute improvements for existing lists and ideas for new ones).

A list of expressions describing infidelity from different languages

5. Scratching in someone else's salad (Afrikaans)

4. Playing outside on a Friday night (Malay)

3. Riding another bicycle (Mexican Spanish)

2. Putting each leg in a different boat (Mandarin)

1. Pouring treasure into foreign laps (Shakespeare)

A list of the time taken to reach fifty million users

8. *Pokémon Go* (19 days)
7. Twitter (2 years)
6. Facebook (3 years—suck it, Facebook)
5. TV (13 years)
4. Radio (38 years)
3. Telephone (50 years)
2. Cars (62 years)
1. Soap and water in male restrooms (any day now)

A list of international OMGs

7. Sprouts! (Italy)
6. Monkeys bite me! (Portugal)
5. I think an elk just kissed me! (Germany)
4. Old Swedish man! (Austria)
3. Take a whole vacation! (Denmark)
2. Drag me backward into a birdhouse! (Norway)
1. Shit yourself, little parrot! (Spain)

A list of foods and the percentage of people that hate them

8. Cilantro (11)
7. Raisins (17)
6. Mushrooms (18)
5. Brussels sprouts (21)
4. Pickles (33)
3. Olives (38)
2. Liver (43)
1. White chocolate (should be 100 because it's a crime against humanity)

A list of maternal insults from around the world

5. Your mother is a big turtle (China)
4. Your mother married a reindeer (Finland)
3. Your mother drinks tap water in Adelaide (Australia)*
2. Your mother is so small her head smells of feet (France)
1. Your mother's navel is an outie (Japan)

---

* And speaking of Australia and mothers: In an Aussie Rules match between St. Kilda and Brisbane Lions, St. Kilda player Brett Voss was about to take a shot at goal when someone shouted, "My old man fucked your mum!" He turned around to find that the player who said it was his brother, Michael, who played for the other team.

A list of Tom Swifties*

8. "My surgery went OK," Tom said, half-heartedly
7. "I don't know what these shoes are laced with," Tom said, tripping
6. "Be quiet while I water down this orange juice," Tom said, concentrating
5. "You'll love my impression of a Siberian dog," Tom said in a husky voice
4. "I've dropped the toothpaste," Tom said, crestfallen
3. "I've given up the Elvis impressions," Tom said expressly
2. "Why must everything be put in numbered order," Tom said listlessly
1. "I know how COVID-19 began," Tom said right off the bat

---

* Tom Swifties are a type of punning using adverbs or adverbial phrases in dialogue attributions.

A list of croakers*

5. "Clare, I'm splitting up with you," Tom declared
4. "I deserve this makeover," Tom explained
3. "I suppose I should put some clothes on," Tom panted
2. "I'm not quite the first person to arrive at your party, am I?" Tom second-guessed
1. "And then they built me a prosthetic penis," Tom remembered

---

* Croakers are similar to Tom Swifties, but the pun in the dialogue attribution is a verb rather than an adverb.

A list of actual titles of celebrity memoirs

7. *Pryor Convictions* (Richard Pryor)
6. *Trowel and Error* (TV gardener Alan Titchmarsh)
5. *Sein Language* (Jerry Seinfeld)
4. *Kiss and Make-Up* (Kiss front man Gene Simmons)
3. *Out of Synch* (NSYNC singer Lance Bass)
2. *Don't Hassel the Hoff* (David Hasselhoff)
1. *Cybill Disobedience* (Cybill Shepherd)

A bonus list of potential titles for celebrity memoirs

5. *Lohan Behold* (Lindsay Lohan)
4. *Biden: My Time* (Joe Biden)
3. *I'll Grant Hugh That* (Hugh Grant)
2. *As I Liv and Breathe* (Liv Tyler)
1. *Hanks for Everything* (Tom Hanks)

A list of words rarely seen without a prefix

8. Gruntled

7. Peccable

6. Advertently

5. Sensical

4. Couth

3. Trepid

2. Combobulated

1. Whelmed

A list of the names for bats (the flying things, not the wooden sticks) from different languages

5. Butterfly of the night (Maltese)
4. Little evening one (Italian)
3. Little fool (Irish)
2. Not a ghoul (Polish)
1. Flutter mouse (German)*

* Much has been made of the danger of consuming bats in the wake of COVID-19, but their spit could actually be beneficial. A protein in the saliva of the *Desmodus rotundus* (vampire bat) is an anticoagulant currently being developed into a medicine (with the snazzy name draculin).

A list of excellent business names

7. Lawn Order (landscapers)
6. Vinyl Resting Place (record store)
5. You Should Be Shot (portrait photographer)
4. Hairy Pop-Ins (pet groomers)
3. Bloodbath & Beyond (gun store)
2. Pulp Friction (juice bar)
1. The Yard (milkshake bar)

A list of the correct order of biscuits*

5. Jaffa cakes†
4. Chocolate bourbons
3. Choco Leibniz (the fancy German ones)
2. Oreos (the chocolate brownie ones)
1. Triple chocolate chip cookies

---

* In the UK, biscuits are what we dunk in our tea, very different from the US biscuits that cowboys have with grits (that's how I like to think of them anyway). There is an ongoing national debate in the UK to determine the best biscuit, with some other favorites including digestives, rich teas, custard creams, and Hobnobs. Obviously, none of them are as good as those on my list.

† There is an even bigger national debate over whether the Jaffa cake (spongey chocolate-coated biscuit with marmalade in the middle) is indeed a biscuit (it is!). The "Jaffa cakes are actually a cake" crowd (who are completely misguided) has all sorts of (ridiculous) arguments for why Jaffas aren't biscuits. They often point to a court case that the original makers, McVitie's, won in the 1990s, which ruled that legally a Jaffa cake is a cake. The litigation itself was simply a response to McVitie's attempt to avoid paying taxes (cakes are subject to a lower value-added tax than biscuits). And please refer to my earlier list of silly laws in the UK to see how often the law can get it wrong. The "Jaffa cakes are cakes" crowd also likes to relentlessly chant that the "the clue is in the name!" By that logic, I trust they're eating urinal cakes with whipped cream on top? Please refer to my list of misnomers for other instances of absurd designations. They may be "technically" a cake in the same way tomatoes are "technically" a fruit (every rational being knows otherwise). Anyway, the fact of the matter is, Jaffa cakes look like biscuits, taste like biscuits, come in biscuit packaging, and are sold in the biscuit aisles of supermarkets. Thus endeth my rant.

A list of books and the time it took to write them

8. Old Testament (1,000 years)
7. *The Catcher in the Rye* (10 years)
6. *Lord of the Flies* (5 years)
5. *1984* (1 year)
4. *Twilight* (3 months)
3. *A Clockwork Orange* (3 weeks)
2. *The Boy in the Striped Pyjamas* (2.5 days)
1. My first novel (I don't mean to brag . . . but watch out Old Testament)

A list of international excuses

7. The bad workman blames his tools (English)

6. A bad wagoner blames the donkeys (Spanish)

5. If the farmer can't swim, it's due to his swimming trunks (German)

4. The skewed rocket is hindered by space (Bulgarian)

3. A heron blames the water because he cannot swim (Danish)

2. An ugly girl blames the mirror (Serbo-Croatian)

1. A poor dancer is impeded by his own balls (Russian)

A list of fun place names

8. Westward Ho! (Devon)
7. Kalamazoo (Michigan)
6. Knobhead (Antarctica)
5. Saint Louis-du-Ha!-Ha! (Québec)
4. Tickle Cock Bridge (Yorkshire)
3. Mianus (Connecticut)
2. Bendova (Czech Republic)
1. Cookie Town (Oklahoma)

A bonus list of translated European place names

5. Chibaovci (Bulgaria) = Go Away Sheep
4. Pungpinan (Sweden) = Scrotum Agony
3. Babina Guzica (Croatia) = Grandma's Ass
2. Swornegacie (Poland) = Not Naughty Pants
1. Saaranpaskantamasaari (Finland) = Island Shat by Sarah

A list of why you shouldn't say "my bosses have given me too much work to do"

3. Boring
2. Whiny
1. Nobody cares

A list of why you should instead use the Hungarian phrase "they chased me into the dick forest with a wide-open mouth"*

3. Cosmopolitan
2. Poetic
1. Very relatable

---

* If you want to be truly cosmopolitan, use the phrase in the original Hungarian: *Bekergettek tátott szájjal a faszerdobe.*

A list of the number of words per language (roughly)

7. Taki Taki (340)
6. Classical Latin (40,000—all boring)
5. Malay (83,000)
4. French (135,000)
3. German (330,000)
2. English (500,000)
1. Pedantese (Depends how you count hyphenated words. Or morphemes/ lexemes. Either way, you're probably wrong)

A list of names for pedants in different countries

5. Comma fucker (Finland)
4. Raisin pooper (Germany)*
3. Ant fucker (the Netherlands)
2. Little dot shitter (Switzerland)
1. Sodomizer of flies (France)

* Another fun German word for a pedant is *Erbsenzaehler* (counter of peas).

A list of actual florist names

7. Florist Gump
6. Austin Flowers
5. Back to the Fuchsia
4. The Lone Arranger
3. Judy's Garlands
2. Floral and Hardy
1. How Mad Is She?

A list of titles of real research papers

5. “Can a Cat Be Both a Solid and a Liquid?” (physics)

4. “The Effect of Country Music on Suicide” (medicine)

3. “Chickens Prefer Beautiful Humans” (interdisciplinary)

2. “Why Do Old Men Have Big Ears?” (anatomy)

1. “Salmonella Excretion in Joy-Riding Pigs” (biology)

A bonus list of the single best title for a research paper ever

1. In March 2006, Professor Daniel M. Oppenheimer published a paper that argued writers seem more intelligent when using simple words than fancy ones. His paper was titled “Consequences of Erudite Vernacular Utilized Irrespective of Necessity”*

* And Oppenheimer should verily be extolled for his utilization of Brobdingnagian lexemes and magniloquent verbosity to manifest a humorously sesquipedalian appellation.

A list of festive celebrities

8. Spruce Willis
7. Demi Moore-Turkey-Anyone?
6. Elf Macpherson
5. Snoop Dogg-Is-for-Life-Not-Just-for-Christmas
4. Wreath Witherspoon
3. Christopher-Walken-in-a-Winter-Wonderland
2. Oprah Wintery
1. Kim Kardashian-through-the-Snow

A list of useful Russian expressions

5. That’s no potato (that’s no laughing matter)

4. Every barber knows that (it’s a badly kept secret)

3. It is understandable to a hedgehog (it’s simple)

2. Here is where the dog is buried (this is the crux of the issue)

1. Rope is good when it’s long, speech is good when it’s short (shut up now)

A list of things that animals simply cannot do

7. Elephants (jump)
6. Crocodiles (move their tongues)
5. Rabbits (vomit)
4. Snow leopards (roar)
3. Lions (purr)
2. Birds (sweat)
1. Humans (keep New Year's resolutions)

A list of ten reasons why I didn't stick to my New Year's resolution

1. Lazy

A list of "They lived happily ever after" in different languages

7. They lived well and we better (Greek)
6. They were happy and ate partridges (Spanish)
5. The tale is over, and the eggplant is boiled (Tamil)
4. Snip, snap, snout, this tale's told out (Norwegian)
3. That was the length of it (Finnish)
2. And if they didn't die, they're still alive today (German)
1. Then along came a pig with a long nose, and the story was over (Flemish)

A list of the five unwritten laws of concluding a book

5.

4.

3.

2.

1.

ABOUT THE AUTHOR

Adam is originally from Manchester, England, but has moved around often (he's not very good at staying still). A list of some of the places where he's lived

8. London
7. Melbourne
6. Sydney
5. Queensland
4. The Channel Islands
3. The Canary Islands
2. Nashville
1. Newcastle upon Tyne

Adam has had over thirty jobs (he's not a very loyal employee either). A list of some of the things he's been paid to do

8. Teaching sports in kindergartens
7. Serving sandwiches in casinos
6. Catching footballs
5. Juggling bottles

4. Washing dishes
3. Reviewing music
2. Changing diapers
1. Walking on stilts

And here, in closing, is a list of Adam's proudest achievements to date

5. Seventh-grade table tennis champion
4. Once almost managed to fold a fitted sheet
3. Taught his granddad to use the internet
2. Going a whole week without saying "that's what she said"
1. This book

You can find Adam on Twitter (and tell him all the things he got wrong in this book) at @AdamCSharp.

ACKNOWLEDGMENTS

A list of people I would like to thank

10. Clare Rees, for all the great advice
9. Northumbria University, for the generous grant to do my PhD with them
8. The JULA team, especially Milly, Donna, and Jo
7. Jenny Knight, my fellow pig phrase enthusiast
6. Everyone at Andrews McMeel Publishing, especially Kevin Kotur
5. Everyone at CookeMcDermid, especially Sally Harding
4. Tobias Biberbach, for helping with my bad German, and Irina Sabatina, for helping with my really bad Russian
3. Maysie and Paul, for the kitchen feedback sessions
2. Kit de Waal, for all the encouragement, inspiration, and friendship
1. The wonderful people who've supported me on Twitter (you know who you are)*

---

* This list is in no particular order because, obsessed as I am with everything being carefully sequenced, ranking people I know is a step too far (just barely).

IMAGE CREDITS

Pages iii, 4 © Getty Images; page viii © Morphart Creation/Shutterstock.com, page 6 © ArtMari/Shutterstock.com, page 7 © alexblacksea/Shutterstock.com, page 9 © Hein Nouwens/Shutterstock.com, page 12 © Artem Musaev/Shutterstock.com, page 17 © LHF Graphics/Shutterstock.com, page 19 © Morphart Creation/Shutterstock.com, page 23 © Morphart Creation/Shutterstock.com, page 24 © Serafima Antipova/Shutterstock.com, page 25 © Mochipet/Shutterstock.com, page 30 © Iriskana/Shutterstock.com, page 31 © sar14ev/Shutterstock.com, page 35 © Hein Nouwens/Shutterstock.com, page 46 © nadiia_oborska/Shutterstock.com, page 49 © Channarong Pherngjanda/Shutterstock.com, page 50 © Serafima Antipova/Shutterstock.com, page 52 © AngryBrush/Shutterstock.com, page 54 © chempina/Shutterstock.com, page 62 © EtherMary and Asahihana/Shutterstock.com, page 71 © olllikeballoon/Shutterstock.com, page 72 © Babich Alexander/Shutterstock.com, page 87 © Hein Nouwens/Shutterstock.com, page 92 © Bodor Tivadar/Shutterstock.com, page 93 © alter711/Shutterstock.com, page 98 © Epine/Shutterstock.com, page 107 © AlexHliv/Shutterstock.com, page 114 © Bodor Tivadar/Shutterstock.com, page 115 © Kamieshkova/Shutterstock.com, page 125 © Hein Nouwens/Shutterstock.com, page 127 © SuperArtWorks/Shutterstock.com, page 131 © Channarong Pherngjanda/Shutterstock.com, page 137 © Babich Alexander/Shutterstock.com, page 148 © Abbie/Shutterstock.com, page 159 © Hein Nouwens/Shutterstock.com, page 167 © Egor Shilov/Shutterstock.com, page 168 © Danussa/Shutterstock.com, page 170 © Melok/Shutterstock.com, page 174 © ArtHeart/Shutterstock.com.